MW01204624

Bookrags Literature Study Guide

Women Who Run With the Wolves by Clarissa Pinkola Estes

Copyright Information

Table of Contents

Plot Summary

This book is written for women by an expert woman in her field. She employs the full spectrum of herself, including her personal life and higher education, followed by experience, to offer women a book about the "Wild Woman" archetype. This is for the sensible task of helping women to have a stronger and clearer sense of identity. Of course, this book can be read by men and boys as well as girls and women. Men might read this book to better understand their Grandma or sister, the mother of their new child, or their lover.

The work contains many stories. The tales contain an assortment of images of the Wild Woman in different age groups and cultures. Rites of passage and initiation are the themes of the stories. Sometimes a rite of passage can take many years, and in other cases it is simply one significant rite.

The author introduces the readers to the "Wild Woman" Archetype. The source material comes from a global range of story traditions; the stories are from both the oral and written tradition. There is a story for every stage of a female's life. Many of the tales show the relationship between one life phase and another, for example, where the elder one initiates the younger. The younger one performs a task or series of tasks to complete the rite of passage.

For those not already aware of the Wild Woman archetype, this book demonstrates numerous ways of understanding this archetype. For those who have felt some stirring, or have had some experience with their own "wildish self," this book will provide their rational and creative minds with more food for thought to further their understanding of self.

Part of the purpose of the book seems to be to provide readers with additional knowledge. However, there is much more to the book's purpose than that, in as much as it constitutes a project to improve the lives of women as a whole by protecting, preserving, and proliferating archetypal knowledge of the Wild Woman. The purposes of the book are all of the above. The book is structured so that those unaccustomed to this type of material will learn not only stories but also be given guidance toward interpreting the stories.

Additionally, the author is preserving her own Latina heritage through this work. She takes steps that other writers have already taken to preserve stories for and about men, when she endeavors to help convert an oral tradition into the written one for its protection and preservation. She is also providing groundwork for women to work with Jungian ideas of the subconscious. While Carl Jung did do a tremendous amount of work with archetypes and with women, he was not able to work on women's archetypes from a female perspective because of the limitation of his time and his gender. As such, Clarissa gifts women with something needed or at the very least, useful.

Women Who Run With the Wolves: Introductory Material & Book 1, The Howl: Resurrection of the Wild Woman Summary and Analysis

The author begins by introducing herself. She makes readers very comfortable by being personal, even through the distance of the written word. One feels befriended by the time the introduction has concluded. Like with a job interview, readers will also feel assured of her qualifications.

Next, the author addresses the pain related resulting from bad experiences, which some of the female population have endured. There are always people who have a better environment in which to thrive, and there are those who have troubles to varying degrees of severity. The author looks at how it has been for those women in America who were not treated well. She then shows how looking to the wild woman archetype can serve a healing function.

One reason for the wild woman archetype is that it portrays a strong and healthy woman. It is a postive view of women rather than the weak, or oppressed view. Estes explains how it is that she was drawn to this archetype herself as part of her bond with nature and with her favorite animal, wolves. She lived through the experience of seeing wolves viewed with fear and hunted to becoming an endangered species. Fortunately, since then, restoration programs have sought to protect this marvelous animal, which, for some, is merely seen as just a menace to farmers.

She tells two tales in the first chapter. One reveals the Wolf Woman, La Loba of the American SouthWest. Old women with the powers of resurrection are the focus of this portion of the story. Bone collecting becomes part of the effort. Ultimately, it shows how an Old Woman alone can find great power and joy in herself and that she holds within herself incredible abilities of transformation. Both the woman and the wolf run free and wild once more at the end of the story. The author is sharing a tale from a living oral tradition.

The other story is remarkably different. It is about four Rabbi who are taken to the Seventh Vault of the Seventh Heaven by an angel of God. While there, they are shown "Ezekial's Wheel." All four are changed by the experience. One went stark raving mad, whose mental illness lasts the rest of his life. Normally, mental illness is temporary but sadly, like broken limbs and influenza, it can recur. Another of the Rabbi spent the rest of his life telling others all about "Ezekial's Wheel" and puzzling over the meaning of the experience. Still another was skeptical to an extreme and belittled the event as having simply been a dream and nothing more. The other Rabbi went on with his life. Although he did not focus much energy directly on the experience with Ezekial's Wheel, he allowed it to transform himself and his life.

The author explains that both stories are about transformation. The second one shows that it is wisest to make neither too much nor too little of transformational experiences. Whether they are external reality, or take place in the inner life, or combinations thereof, they remain significant. Too much or too little attention to the experience or attention at the wrong times can be less than helpful, but taken the right way and at the proper time, such experiences are excellent for the individual, and by changing one person, the world is changed through the ripple effects upon others.

Chapter 1, Stalking the Intruder: The Beginning Initiation Summary and Analysis

Here the author introduces another story. This time, the story is about a man, who has some peculiar characteristic that indicates something else about him. In this sense, it is a bit like a mark, such as when people feared birth marks were an indication of strangeness. In this story, the man mysteriously has a blue beard. Why this is no one knows, but the story clearly indicates that he has not simply dyed the beard blue. It is also impossible for him to hide it.

In the story, the man courts three sisters at the same time. The young women find him frightening due to his strangely-colored beard. As a consequence, they run from him and hide. He entices them into spending time with him, hoping that it will alter their perception. He organizes a party with a feast, which they attend. They have fun and the desired affect is achieved.

Even so, when they are at home again later, the elder sisters grow suspicious once more. They both decide to opt out of the courting relationship with him. However, the youngest decides to go ahead and continue to be involved with the man called Bluebeard.

Although the reason is never clearly explained, there is a rumor that Bluebeard is a "failed magician." This seems to indicate something else about his reputation. Evidently, he has some power but something may have gone wrong. Perhaps he was like the sorcerer's apprentice and tried to go past his limits, but there were troubling consequences.

Pinkola Estes shows readers how this is all designed to show the difference between the naive daughter, who is the youngest and the elder sisters. Clarissa does not go into why the man courted all three sisters at the same time. When girls grow up, especially as they pass through adolescence, there is an enormous amount of education required that directly pertains to how to deal with men. It is also clear that in this story, the girls' father does not figure in the situation. Guidance is given to the youngest from the older sisters, not the

10

parents.

She shows in this chapter how the Wild Woman emerges through curiosity, and sometimes through breaking rules established perhaps by someone who has no right to be the the authority in the woman's life. It is also about a woman's overcoming of her own naivete through subverting authority to the discovery of important but undesirable knowledge.

The youngest sister is endangered, however, by knowledge forbidden to her by Bluebeard. Of course, it was this knowlege, and not the blue beard, that the girl's sisters had sensed correctly earlier in the story. Again, this reflects the need for females, as part of their maturation process, to discern and cultivate subtle and not-so-subtle levels of awareness, especially regarding male behavior. Establishing boundaries is critical as well as the knowledge and understanding of how to relate with each individual man. The emphasis is on the contradictory nature of the information giver, in this case, the man Bluebeard.

At the end of the story, she cries out, not to her sisters, but to her brothers for their physical protection. Her brothers do come to her rescue, and through an unbridled violent struggle with Bluebeard, kill him. It was either that, or their adversary was going to kill their younger sister for finding out that he had murdered his previous wives. Apparently, he could not hide that he was this kind of murderer.

The bad news is that the young woman becomes endangered but discovers the danger through playing with her female siblings and by breaking the one "rule" that her new husband had "given to her." In the story, she does not even intentionally strive to be any kind of rule breaker but was simply caught up in the joyful spontaneity of curiosity-satiating explorations with her sisters. The rest of the bad news is that in order to be saved from this life-threatening predicament, she genuinely needed assistance. Her vulnerability as a tender, young woman, and as a woman who was not a fearsome warrior were double reasons why she was in jeopardy. It took warriors willing and able to engage in a dangerous struggle to the death, to defeat her husband, who was a real warrior.

The story is about the real dangers of female naivete, especially with respect to men. It shows through her male siblings that men who are not lovers and yet are close to her, do care and are often able to sense what is really going on. Thanks to this, they are able to save her life, even though they face the pain and gore of violence and death when they act to protect her. The story shows that instincts and intuitions are generally to be trusted, and that some intuition often comes through education. It also makes it clear that one must guard against dismissing one's hunches, as they are often correct.

Chapter 3, Nosing Out the Facts: The Retrieval of Intuition as Initiation Summary and Analysis

This chapter continues the lessons about being a woman. The tone is one of friendly education. Estes mixes the objective with the subjective. She is not unprofessional in doing so; indeed, her personal tone is very endearing when contrasted with more formal writing styles that often eradicate a sense of the author's personality or identity. This personal writing is also beneficial since it helps readers to cultivate a clear sense of what biases the author has.

This story begins with a family and a tragedy. A girl's mother dies while the girl is in late prepubescent childhood. However, the woman gives the daughter a parting gift--a small doll and urges her daughter to trust in the parting token and to keep it hidden. The child and her father survive this grievous circumstance.

The father re-marries a widow who had daughters. The mother and daughters establish a reign of cruelty against the other woman's child, to which the father remains oblivious and the girl submits. The child hopes that her kindness will transform the others, but, instead, it only makes matters worse. The good news is that the girl is forced to develop in other ways because of how they make her do work.

At some point, the other females conspire to send the more mature, but still very, young girl off, they hope, to her death and demise. They mask their lethal intentions under the guise of a quest to rekindle the family hearth. This is a bit like World War II soldiers being sent to the Russian front. In the story they have not mastered fire-making, so in order to rekindle fire, they have to seek elsewhere until they find some and transport "starter fire." They send the girl to the witch Baba Yaga, who is representative of one type of the Wild Woman archetype. This archetype is the Old Woman, who is intimidating, no longer sexually vibrant, no longer fecund, but with the profound wisdom that comes with age, when experience is properly attended to. Baba Yaga is still energetic and healthy; there is no certainty whether or not she is sexually active, but she is presented as single. This emphasizes her independent condition, but, in truth, does not rule out her having a mate.

The girl goes bravely onward and continues to heed her mother's advice, listening frequently to the little doll that she is still carrying. She meets the witch and finds that she can have what she wants, but she must be willing to trade for it with her labor. There is fear, adventure and a series of 8 tasks. She is not taught fire-starting, but instead is sent with a skull upon a staff that harbors fire. Perhaps this is a metaphor of the female reproductive aspect.

She makes it back home, and her staff reduces her wicked sisters and stepmother to cinders. The author uses this to show readers how sometimes maturation is hard won and frightening, and there are times when it pays off to not be nice, whether we like this truth or not. Not always being nice is sometimes necessary when the adolescent transition causes girls to change and overthrow certain oppressive aspects of their relationships with siblings and parents, even in rather normal families.

The author shows readers many aspects of the Wild Woman in this story. The main character is the innocent "Wild Girl," bearing intuitions that are protective, and powerful guides, even when small and nearly helpless. The tendency towards obedience in an effort to be treated properly or better through pleasing others with correctness and kindness is shown. The reason for this is that under many conditions this is an effective strategy. The harsh truth is that there are those who attack the kind for their very gentleness until or unless those kind ones become aggressive. The Wild Woman is also shown as mother: the too-good mother, but also the absent mother, whose love and guidance are somehow still there. The doll, of course, shows that the mother knew when she died that life would be difficult for her daughter. She tries to give the daughter a gift of comfort, but also something to empower and to guard their connection with one another.

The Old Woman, the Grandmother Witch, ends up training the girl. Instead of destroyed, the girl receives initiation and training. Once that has been completed, she returns to her family as a powerful being. The other females fail to keep her entirely away from her father. She has a rightful place there. When she gets back, she is more powerful and more mature than she was before. She conquers the opponents who used to dominate her. Finally, this is also clearly the heroine's journey;

it may be less soldierly and violent than the story of male maturation, but the same elements of innocence, transformation, gender roles, wisdom, and courage, which challenges and overcomes powerful hostility from others are present.

Chapter 4, The Mate: Union With the Other
Summary and Analysis

This chapter seems somehow deceptive. The author carries on in a tone that blends her roles both as a story teller and a practicing psychologist. The story is nonfiction and objective but is interwoven with the power of story telling. The stories include falsehoods in a design that reveals additional truths. An analogy to this is the way that people can hide and reveal and express themselves through attire.

The first story is named Manawee. Here a man (Manawee) is courting a set of twin daughters. This fellow is not like Bluebeard. The twins have a protective father, who interferes by making it clear that if Manawee is interested in the twins as wives, then he is going to have to put forth the effort to discover their true names. The true name is something that belongs to many traditions. Often it was used in families in association with mysteries. The true name is often hidden because knowledge of it was seen as giving great power to those who knew one's true name. This works well as a metaphor to those who do not have this idea in their religious tradition. The father simply wants the man to be interested in the true essence of his daughters: the man's interest needs to be deep.

The man comes and goes. He repeatedly attempts to meet the young women, only to be sent away by the father. After a bit, the man's little dog goes and visits the twins on his own. Unlike the man, the pet does not run into the same problems and quickly learns the true names of the women Manawee hopes to marry as the pair that they have always been. This is about the value of instincts and of observations. The dog can do freely what the man cannot, but the dog and the man are connected. The girls trust the dog and the dog trusts the girls and Manawee.

The dog runs into a similar, but worse problem, than the man. He gets further and in fact learns the true names of the sisters because he hears them calling one another by name. Being the innocent animal that he is, he has no difficulty getting close to them, and the girls are quite kind

16

to him. The dog's problem is that he receives the correct information but is repetitiously waylaid during his efforts to return to his human Master. By the time he gets back, he has forgotten the information. However, he is a persevering sort of animal and so he actually tries again. This happens to him several times, but after a number of attempts, the dog decides against pursuing attractive alternatives in an effort to preserve the valuable information that he is harboring. In the end, after multiple attempts, the dog succeeds in bringing the information to the man.

By the time Manawee turns up bearing the information that will satisfy their father, the twins are awaiting him as a unit to be his wives. This reveals the natural mutuality of the relationship between Manawee and the twins, while it also indicates that somehow the situation was and was not as it appeared on the surface to be. It also shows that the father's request only served to make it so that the three younger people would learn to either drop the matter or else to follow through. If they did so well enough, then the three would naturally become well prepared to be married with the enduring kind of real love.

Chapter 5, Hunting: When the Heart is a Lonely Hunter Summary and Analysis

This chapter carries a story that relates directly to what the author describes as the Life/Death/Life cycle. The story of the chapter is about a happy romance, except that it is a very sad and scary story about a person called Skeleton Woman. Skeleton Woman began as a living woman, who suffered brutally from her father. In many versions of the story, she is killed off by him; whereas, in other forms of the same tale, she suffers having her hands cut off and other atrocities. Destroyed, she sinks to the bottom of a body of water and her flesh rots away. Nothing happens for a very long time. There are versions of the story when this occurred as a form of punishment, and other tales when she suffers because of her father's behavior.

One day, a fisherman cheerfully roams into the area above where her skeleton rests, and when he casts his line, he hooks Skeleton Woman. He believes he has caught a large fish and is happily bringing it aboard. Instead, he pulls up the skeletal remains of a woman murdered by her own father. He is horrified and possibly disgusted when he finds he has snagged the remains of a murder victim, instead of enough food for weeks. He tries to escape this terrible new knowledge by dumping the skeleton, but it doesn't work. He is unable to get rid of the skeleton; in his fear and hurry, he ends up dragging the skeletal remains along. Innocent of having caused her death in any way, he is nevertheless now bound to it; in running away, he causes the bones to bounce, rattle and jump along. While rattling along behind, something happens to skeleton woman. Somehow she takes in nourishment despite being nothing but the bony remnants of a corpse. This occurs as she is being dragged by the man's fishing line as he does his best to flee from her at the time.

He retreats into the safety of his home but finds that he has dragged the skeleton woman in there with him. He confronts his fear in a new way-- by calming down and becoming more patient. He puts the skeleton in order and then he rests. While the exact telling of the tale may vary, what happens is that during the night when he is asleep, skeleton woman transforms from Death back into Life and becomes this man's lover. She slips into bed with him, unopposed. When they awake in the morning, the two are refreshed and find themselves both alive and intertwined.

The author explains that she sees similar real-life events metaphorically playing out in numerous clients' lives in her role as professional psychologist. As a Jungian analyst, she sees the Life of the woman destroyed by her father and the remains lay fallow. Involvement in a romance with a lover or intimate relationship with a man, brings back this whole Life/Death/Life cycle. She shares with readers that she teaches clients that they are handling Skeleton Woman but tending to project it upon their new partner. She posits that when people strive to avoid or run from relationships that they are coping with what relating to another has confronted them. This needs to be faced. It is not actually caused by the relationship but with what each person is coming to terms.

Chapter 6, Finding One's Pack: Belonging as Blessing Summary and Analysis

This chapter begins with a classical fairy tale with which most readers will likely be familiar. The story starts with a strange egg. There is no confusion: it is evident that this egg is different from the very beginning. There are guesses made by other mature creatures about what the egg is.

Some bizarre creature emerges from the egg and even the mother is unable to hide this. She strives to protect the entity anyways, but the so-called duckling does not fit in, which is what the mother and the duckling both fear--both want the young creature to be accepted. The dual energies of the mother wishing to nurture and protect this offspring and her own struggle and misfortune due to the undeniable peculiarity of her oddball offspring both occur in the story.

Hazing, harassment, and sorrow expose the cruelties related to ostracism as a method of regulating behavior. When the mother gives up on the duckling after her own struggles on his behalf, the entity runs away.

Unfortunately, life does not suddenly become fabulous just because the juvenile has fled the misery of painfully not fitting in. The author points out that this problem affects the entire family. Not only that, but the whole community is affected. The duckling story is equally applicable whether a male or female entity. The community may well be relieved when the duckling flees. The duckling goes on in sorrowful resignation. He seeks shelter and sometimes finds it. Other times he faces the changing elements. Cold and ice frighten the growing "duckling."

Good fortune sometimes occurs, such as when a human farmer rescues the creature from the ice, but then, when the family of humans attempt to care for this wild animal, it does not go well. Humor, drama, and chaos ensue until the growing young being flees yet another situation; however, the creature has changed. Now, it has great enough trust of humans to effectively find shelter repeatedly and thereby survives the winter despite the the quality of care given the young duckling.

One day, after surviving this way for some time, the animal dares to approach some other water fowl. Given previous experiences, the creature predicts a rather negative reaction from the others; however, the others are very friendly and react in a new way. This unusual response is an extremely good one. The entity finds itself being treated well by these others. There is no doubt this is preferred, even though it feels odd due to having received so much bad treatment in the past.

Soon the creature discovers there is a very good reason for this intense sense of belonging. Upon viewing its own reflection in the water, this entity sees that it has become a swan. The answer is simple: it is accepted by the others because it looks like the others, who are also swans. No longer an ugly duckling among ducks or humans, it is now a swan amongst swans. This changes everything--the swan adjusts to the pleasurable reality that he or she finally fits in.

The author then goes on to make a survey of a variety of ways that females, especially, face challenges relating to fitting in or not. It occurs in a multiplicity of ways at more than one phase of their lives. She talks about many of these. She refers to the exile, which can be either voluntary or involuntary.

Of course, in the end, this chapter shows a twofold nature to fitting in after having not done so for such a very long time. One has learned much from being different; once there is the joyous healing of belonging, the experiences of finding a "fit" will make life even more gratifying.

Chapter 7, Joyous Body: The Wild Flesh Summary and Analysis

Clarissa begins this chapter with additional observations that she has made about wolves, who are such a favorite with her that they are akin to being her "totem" animal. She follows this with a re-discovery of the female body and how we can enjoy, celebrate and accept our bodies. She also shows some of the psychological ways that women's bodies have come under attack. She is not referring to criminal forms of assault, but nasty, mental methods designed to reduce natural, healthy love and self-confidence that is the innate nature of females.

In the sub-sections of this chapter, the author shares more of her own life. During "Body Talk," she describes how a woman friend and she celebrated and healed themselves with an on-stage production. She further explores the healing of one's self-image in "The Body in Fairy Tales." Here, instead of obsessions regarding body types, readers receive some history of the secret worlds of those who have delved into such things as talismans, magic, mystics, magic carpets and dreams. She argues the possibility for the body to be a great storehouse of wisdom, rather than being opposed to the spiritual.

The author takes readers into a new celebration of one of the most profound changes in a female's adult life: the discovery of the power of fertility as direct personal experience, in contrast to knowledge of it gleaned from the outside. She rediscovers the beauty of the female form from the position of strength. In this section, rather than being a source of shame or denigration, any and all markings left by the experience of pregnancy and child birth are perceptually transformed into icons of natural female power that has been unleashed. Life emerges. Taoists call women "the gateway" largely because whether male or female, everyone enters life through a woman's womb.

She completes this look at the female body with the brilliance of the unexpected. La Mariposa, the Butterfly Woman turns out to be a generously-proportioned grandmother, rather than a lithe young, but full grown, maiden. Estes observes that all the prohibitions against touching others have been released in part, since the grandmother has passed menopause and graduated from a number of the major preoccupations of a woman's life.

The Wild Woman, the author assures readers is available at every stage of life, whether in form of a mentor or as a spirit that is inherent within the female herself. In this chapter, more of the Wild Woman's aspects are found, as are ways to connect with her--how she can heal and other powers she has. The Wild Woman visions in this chapter are kinder and gentler than the Baba Yaga readers met earlier.

Chapter 8, Self-Preservation: Identifying Leg Traps, Cages, and Poisoned Bait Summary and Analysis

Here the author adds to the images of women and the Wild Woman with still more stories. She brings the notion of a "feral woman" into focus. She defines feral as wild and untamed. She writes of how all women are born this way, and yet how often much gets lost or injured during the civilizing process, whether during childhood or as an adult. She refers to the deep healing involved when women find ways to save their souls, not as a religious project, but as a kind of personal-reclamation project. This includes resuming to be, or to harbor within themselves, what it means for a woman to be "Wild," or at the very least rather natural as opposed to cultured to a point of pained artificiality.

For those who have been thriving, this section will be like watching or hearing of the painful stories of hurt women. It about a kind of strange twisting of something, probably the soul of an individual. In this story, a girl is financially poor, but rich, through her own resourcefulness and her own ignorance of what she might be missing. She makes a pair of her own shoes; she has been industrious, responsible, creative, self-expressive, and even practical.

She is taken in by wealth, but whether it is the middle class, the rich, or simply civilization through schooling and the learning of "proper manners" is not made explicitly clear. Her shoes are destroyed by a kind of clinical, sterilized brand of evil masquerading as benevolence. It is a starched collar type of Old Woman. The girl's natural spirit is heavily assaulted by the conditions, even though the relative elegance is attractive.

She ends up getting to have red shoes again, but there is something wrong about them. The ones she receives later in the story are not coming directly from her soul but are a corrupted form of what she really desires; however, the new ones match her true memory of her original shoes and life plan in color but their form represents precisely "what the Devil wanted:" they are pricier and made by others. Her life ends up destroyed by this artificial substitute. Ironically, the Old Woman who destroyed her original red shoes, is consistent in that she is equally opposed to the girl getting the substitutes. One cannot be sure whether the Old Woman was right or whether it was the Old Woman's hostility even towards the higher-class, civilized version of the shoes that, combined with a man playing the Devil in the disguise of a retired soldier, turned the new shoes into the "evil destructive force" that they became. In the story it is because of a man tapping the shoes that the destructive and uncontrollable form of them is unleashed.

This is a very creepy tale. Readers hold out hope that the girl who had her hopes dashed is finally going to get her own life back. Readers hope that her new social knowledge will help her to thrive again. At first, it seems to work, but then, some kind of curse emerges making what had become her release into a dreadful prison of its own.

In the end, she has her feet cut off and then serves others. There is more than one way to interpret this story. Estes' version is that psychologically, readers should imagine the girl regrowing her feet. This is important to understand the therapeutic intentions and approach to the author's work. She often refers to her actual practice as a psychologist in reference to the stories in the book.

Part of what is being taught is that development includes a long process of initiation. In an earlier chapter, Estes has introduced the awareness that often initiation is a multi-step process. There are often a set of tasks that must be completed in order to arrive. In this chapter, she uses a similar, orderly process to show psychological problem areas from which some women suffer. Although disturbing, the purpose of showing how and where trouble can emerge is to help women find the precise location of where they need healing or how to be able to tell how to evade some difficulty.

The author both saddens and frightens women during this part of the chapter. The reason is that for all those women who had been mentally free, some of this information reminds readers of painful or sad ideas or bad experiences that they themselves had and they may feel a sense of hopelessness when they understand that the woman with the red shoes lives the rest of her life with no feet. On the good side, the author also cites numerous ways women can find healing, even when we look deeply into some of the pain that women can undergo in life. The idea that we are all in this together adds a dimension of relief through participating in sharing the pain, even when that problem was someone else's.

As she is a psychologist, Estes points to how the self-preservation instincts can function properly or get injured, and how to heal them, and also how to recognize symptoms of damage or other trouble. How this affects readers depends on what they are looking for. To use an athletic analogy: If you had hoped this was going to be about running, but instead, there is a discourse about what causes sprained or broken ankles and shin splints and what to do about those conditions; well, it may be unpleasant reading, but may be helpful knowledge.

The wildish woman, when whole will not suffer from addictions; however, any such problems might be a sign of the natural woman crying out. The author shows quite a spectrum of the possibilities for how women can protect herself, but this includes a great deal of learning, along with trust in her natural instincts. However a woman must learn to heal and to guard the innate wisdom of those instincts in order to allow them to help, rather than endanger the civilized woman.

Chapter 9, Homing: Returning to Oneself Summary and Analysis

Here the author uses yet another story to introduce a complex process that can be part of the female experience. The main story is about a painfully lonely man who finds a woman. However, she is not an ordinary woman at all; in fact, she is a seal-woman. This means that her normal form is that of a seal, but unlike ordinary seals, she can emerge from the water and actually transform into the shape of a human woman. This makes her like some of the merfolk because she can function on land as a human. The man's plight is simple: without other companionship, he is even more keen to find a mate. What he would have done were he not lonely remains unknown, but the truth is that he was acutely so.

What is so challenging about this story is that the lonely man finds a woman who is a seal much of the time. However, he needs a woman so desperately that he strikes a deal with her. While there is no violent capture involved, the man is somehow so assertive that he persuades her to try 7 years of her life with him. If she does not wish to stay after that, she can leave him. She goes along with it and they have a child together.

However, by the time those 7 years are up, she has suffered from a worsening condition that the author explains as the intense need to return to her seal self and the water. In the story, it is her son who manages to find her "seal-skin," which is her "native soul," and he returns it to her.

She ends up having to make another agreement with the man for custodial arrangements in the best interests of all of them. It is very noticeable that the terms arrived at are not caused by any malice or bitterness but reflect an honest assessment of the situation, including the needs of each of them. The boy learns of the powers he inherited from his mother and visits her homeland with her. Then he returns to his father, and she goes back to the sea but promises to come back for visits to both the boy and the husband if possible.

The author explains that every woman has her own "seal skin"--what she refers to as the "soul skin." This is the true self. While no woman has to be separated from it, some will find that events can transpire where they are forced to adapt and go without the "soul skin." The "skin," or some other symptom. will appear sooner or later, sending her a message that she needs to return home. The need is so intense that by returning, she literally saves her own spiritual and physical life and also her psychological being.

Pinkola Estes exhorts women to either "stay home" or to learn to "go back to it" (their "soul skin") during their lives as an imperative and integral part of the adult lifestyle. She explains to readers that one does not necessarily need a divorce or separation in order to "return home" but that some method of doing this is powerful protection of a woman's well being.

Chapter 10, Clear Water: Nourishing the Creative Life Summary and Analysis

In this case the author does not begin with a story so much as a description of another concept that is part of a healthy woman's life. This chapter is devoted to the flow of creative forces that a woman has and uses. She refers to these natural powers as "a river" and water is used to symbolize what is an "essential property that vitalizes inert materials into life when combined with them in just the right way."

There is a very sad story in this chapter about another woman from the Latina traditions. She is called La Llorona which translates as "The Weeping Woman." This is a love story about a conflict of values that leads a woman into a painful situation. In this case. a woman and a man are in love with one another, although not married to each other. They have a couple of children out of wedlock and are raising them together as a family and all is well.

Until suddenly things cease to good for the woman. This is because the man either ends up showing that he does not love her as she had believed or wished to believe or if he does love her, he has been heavily influenced by a conflict of values. He informs her that he is off to his native Spain to marry someone his family has selected for him. He tells her that he is taking their children with him.

She is horrified. In one version of the story, she attacks him with violence and herself as well, hurting them physically in the same way that this hurts them emotionally to "conform to the social order." In every version of this story, this woman is rather innocent in that she is simply the victim of abandonment. However in at least one version, this abandonment leads her to become fearsomely destructive and she kills her children rather than giving them up to their father and losing them that way.

Later La Llorono herself commits suicide. She is raised to the gates of heaven but is sent back down by a Saint, who tells her that must go and gather up the souls of her children and bring them back with her in order to get in. In the end, this process remains incomplete, and she can be seen searching the river for the souls of her children.

In another version, the woman does not commit violence, but a clean river ends up being polluted. Then, cleaning the river becomes a major project likened to the image of La Llorona scouring the bottom for her offspring, weeping. Estes tells readers that safeguarding the creativity in a woman's life is much like protecting the river and La Llorona. Was the Weeping Woman naive? We do not know, but regardless of whether or not she was, the same consequences follow. When the waters are pure, there is plenty of life in the river. Whether a woman expresses her life-giving powers mainly through offspring or via alternative creative forms, guarding their impurities and cleansing them should they become polluted is part of the task. There is great sorrow in "lifelessness."

Chapter 11, Heat: Retrieving Sacred Sexuality Summary and Analysis

The heroine in this chapter is a goddess named Baubo, whose image is a grown woman's torso. Her genitals speak, and she sees the world through the nipples of her bosom. She is very witty; her humor is based in the sexually-mature perspective on life. What one might or might not have expected was that the comedy of Baubo is what rescues the mighty mother goddess from depression. Even though Demeter is a powerful goddess, she was despondent from her zealous, but fruitless efforts, to find her daughter, Persephone. Persephone had been taken by Hades, the god of the Underworld.

The goddess Demeter could rescue her daughter from the clutches of this Underworld god who had taken her, with the help from other deities, but found no help there. She grew very sad and her sorrow worsened into real depression after her intent efforts had failed for some time. She feared for her grown child's well being. She may well have also feared that the daughter would think that her mother or anyone didn't care.

The now very dirty-from-searching goddess Demeter sank into a depression. Her sadness was so extreme that she turned very destructive. She ran around crying out, "Die! Die! Die!" and so powerful was her feeling that the vegetation died and Winter set in. Later, still miserable she rested by the side of a well, where she was approached by another goddess. It was Baubo, the adult female torso-shaped goddess who entertained Demeter so effectively and extensively with sexual humor that the power of the Demeter's laughter released her from the depression that had set in.

The great renewal that came from this ensured the success of recovering Persephone. In the end, she did find and rescue her daughter. To do so, she needed to add to her own renewed powers (thanks to Baubo), with those of the goddess Hekate and the Sun god Helios.

Chapter 12, Marking Territory: The Boundaries of Rage and Forgiveness Summary and Analysis

The story in this chapter is about a war veteran and his wife. Apparently, the two were married or at least a couple before the man went off to war. The trouble was that when he came back, he had changed. He showed a number of emotional problems that had impacted his behavior and it was a different man.

The woman loved him just as she always had. She made efforts to show this to him in the usual ways but the changes in his personality kept causing problems. She continued to make efforts to show him affection, being rather patient and persistent with him. His behavior was so odd that she found herself trying things such as bringing him food outdoors where he had taken to sleeping. While off at war, he had slept under the stars a great deal to such an extent that he had grown rather accustomed to it.

For the woman, or for both of them, there was more difficulty--he frightened her. He did not attack her or anything like that, but he was often beset by rage. He would get very surly and she tended to shy away as a result. This bothered her because she loved him very much and wanted to resolve this dilemma. So she went to a healer.

The older woman healer was able to reassure the younger woman that this difficulty could be overcome and that her husband could be cured of the strange, new frightening behaviors. She listened intently for the healer's instructions. Effectively, she was sent on a quest to fetch one body hair from a wild animal, male or female and one body hair from the throat of the Crescent Moon Bear.

The wife showed the determination of her love by facing her tremendous fear and went ahead and set off on the journey. In order to achieve this, she had to leave her husband and climb a mountain where the chances of finding one of these bears was good. This quest took quite some time in and of itself and was full of challenges, but, nevertheless, it was quite clear the woman was making progress.

After a long time, she made it to an area where there actually was a Crescent Moon Bear dwelling in its natural habitat. She was naturally frightened and intimidated; however she wished to achieve her goal and sought a safe way to do so. She had brought food with her and decided to try on the bear the same as she had done with her husband upon his return: She put out a food offering near the bear and kept herself to a safe distance. The bear sniffed the breezes and the food, probably quite sensitive despite its massive size. The bear was able to feel safe enough to enjoy the food offering without needing to seek out or hunt down the source of the new human odor associated with the offering.

This cycle was repeated and the woman made steady progress to gaining the bear's trust. As the process worked, the woman was able to get quite close to the bear without being attacked, and the animal would still eat the food that she gave him. Ultimately, this system was so effective that she was able to ask the bear for one hair from the fur on its throat. The bear allowed this and they parted as soon as this task was achieved.

She made her way back home, triumphant and having grown from her experiences. What was shocking was that when she finally brought the magic hair to the healer so that she could have the healing potion for her husband, the older woman took the hair and then just cast it into her fireplace, where it burned to nothing almost instantly. After that, the healer told the woman to go home to her husband and apply what she learned from her journey and she was sure to succeed.

While no mention is made of how much the soldier may have healed on his own thanks to the extra time and space he was given by his wife, the wife's journey is seen as a heroine's journey.

The author discusses this type of healing. She also tells readers about rage, and that "having tea with it" and learning from it can be helpful. Note that this is not the same as nurturing the anger itself so it grows bigger and stronger, but rather nurturing the being so the rage can be what it is--part of the system of self-respect. She offers a few informal healing techniques.

The second story in the chapter is about a man whose rage led him to commit excessive and often inappropriate acts of violence. He was aware of this and the problem bothered him. Fed up with the havoc his own "rage demon" had caused him, he sought advice from an elder. The Old Man told him to go to an oasis that was in bad condition and keep to himself and be a kind servant to whomever showed up. In other words give water from the oasis to travelers. The man did this for years and it helped him immensely.

Then one day, another stranger turned up and for some reason the situation "turned around" and suddenly the man who had been sitting at the oasis killed the other. Afterwards, he began to experience regret and confusion. After all this time, he had thought he had made progress and believed his rage had really subsided. Now, suddenly, he had killed again. He began to feel both sorrow and shame about this when suddenly another rider appeared. "Thank you!" the other man told him, and then explained that the one he had just killed had been intent upon assassinating the king of their land. The man who had killed him felt very relieved that his ferocity and violence had not been out of place in this case. This was extremely reassuring, but he still felt a little confused.

The basic idea of this chapter is about learning to honor legitimate rage. Whether individually felt or felt as a collective, there is a sense to rage. Despite its bad reputation, it is designed to be a great protector of each of us. It is only when something has "gone awry" that it gets out of control. At the same time, it is equally important to keep in mind that any efforts to kill off healthy rage or the source of it are misguided. It does not serve the best interests of a woman or man to "de-claw" themselves or to endeavor to destroy the rage that is the guardian of their very life, even though the rage may be occasionally misdirected.

Chapter 13, Battle Scars: Membership in the Scar Clan Summary and Analysis

This chapter presents something that on the surface is unrelated but at a closer look, it is connected with the more overt forms of aggression--it is the delicate and sometimes vicious art of secrecy.

Clarissa Pinkola Estes tells readers about secrets and how they can affect peoples' lives in general. She associates them with tears. She explains how it is that somehow secrets often have a structure to them. She writes that while there are heroic tales, there are other tales that run more to the tragic. Either way, she shows that in real life, many travails follow the pattern of drama as found in the theatre, possibly because art imitates life as much or more than life imitates art. As a psychologist, Estes expresses that sharing a secret (something which you are ashamed to tell anyone else about yourself), and also writing down the secret and imagining a happier or preferred ending, which she does with a few of the fairy tales in this book, are all healthy ways to manage experience and feelings associated with events.

She includes the challenge of addressing shame when recounting secrets. For women, many painfully-kept secrets seem to include some manner of "double bind"--often someone did something that has a lot of shame associated with it and someone else or that person (in addition to the victim) is bearing a lot of shame about the situation. There is the need to release the secret and the shame, and there is fear associated with exposing the shame associated with the events that has been being carried by someone, often by someone in silence.

The author encourages seeking psychoanalysis for the relief of the shame of holding a secret. She says that hiding or trying to cover shame is often counter-productive. She says that getting this stuff out in the open is important, although most people might find that they feel awkward about this; it is a bit too much like showing someone the contents of the toilet immediately after you've used it but before you flush. Once you get over that hesitation, you'll be okay. Even so, that isn't what shame is exactly but it does need to be exposed. The idea with shame and secrets is that, like vampires, they will burn up on contact with the light of day.

Finally, in this chapter, Estes assures readers that freeing themselves from keeping the wrong sorts of secrets will offer great rewards. People have often been tricked or manipulated into keeping a secret whether to preserve a good reputation, or a bank roll or just Mommy's approval. She explains that mentally and emotionally, people may suffer from areas where they lack feeling. She offers an analogy that this lack of feeling is not so much because the muscles in their backsides were deadened from being in a chair for so long, but because the secret keeper was so strongly dissuaded from admitting to, acknowledging, owning up to or otherwise "airing something out" for so long. The example of a kept secret that Estes gives is one about a woman, whose husband had committed suicide, had been treated extremely badly by the in-laws long before the husband died. The parents didn't want to admit and did not want her to admit that their cruelty to him might have had some part in his death. It helped this woman tremendously when she finally did talk about that.

Ultimately the conclusion to be drawn from this chapter is for women to acknowledge and appreciate what the author calls "the ovarios" of women. What women have done; what women have been through; it all matters, and women can recognize and honor the "scars" and battles they came from as integral to the lives of women on the whole.

Chapter 14, La Selva Subterranea: Initiation in the Underground Forest Summary and Analysis

In this chapter, the author begins with a term from psycho-therapy-- "projective identification." She introduces the idea of how stories must have a receptive mind in order to make an impact. By the end of this chapter, Estes applies a technique that she has already interpretively used. Estes points out, though, that even with the interpretations offered about the following story, one must avoid the foolhardy, unhealthy fantasizing of which the Little Match Girl indulged.

A father accidentally sells out his own daughter to the Devil for material wealth. He does not do so intentionally, and would not have noticed but for the fact that his wife pointed out to him what he had agreed to do. The parents are truly sad about what they have done, and yet they do not alter their course of action once they have made the deal. It's a sort of "the deed is done; we've made the deal; our word is good so there's no going back" situation.

The daughter is extraordinary. Not only is she young, pure and innocent, but she has cultivated or simply inherently an intense connection with the spiritual realm. Thanks to her power in this regard, the simple fact that she is either not sexually attracted to the Devil or that she is not interested in him triggers a powerful blast of energy that hurls him away from her.

He negotiates with her parents in an effort to turn the daughter into a person he can be involved with, especially since he is so taken by her and having her is his part of the bargain. Despite his powers of evil and darkness, he continues to be unable to force her into intimacy with him or to take possession of her. The parents and the devil try filth, and it helps, but her crying is so cleansing that the diabolic force is instantly repelled. Later, to their shared horror, she is maimed: Her own father cuts off her hands in an effort to make her acceptable to the Devil and weak enough of spirit or flesh as to make her appealing to him. Not even that works. The Devil gives up, or appears to, but the mortals do not lose because they tried to keep their part of the bargain, but the father had intended to give up one apple tree and had not ever wished to lose his daughter over this.

The father offers to financially support the daughter throughout her adult life in a luxurious and affectionate manner. She thanks him sincerely but tells her parents that she must have a go at living as a beggar to find out what it is like to be wholly dependent upon the goodness of others for sustenance and protection. She wanders off to do this and is accompanied by the same spirit that was able to "toss the Devil." There are a few other miraculous or paranormal events surrounding the woman, typically due to this particular spirit in her. The woman is so sensitive that she is able to receive food from a tree because the tree offers it to her; hence, she did not ask and violate the terms of her "beggership," which she had devised.

It turns out that the pear tree belongs to a king; he is a living man and his title is not mere fantasy, but he is located in the underworld. This man asks his magician and his gardener whether the young woman with the strange superpowers is a spirit or a mortal. His magician explained that she is both at once. The king falls in love with her rather instantly and is to be commended for the easy way that he accepts this about himself and her. He courts her. Unlike the Devil, this man meets no resistance. Soon enough, they are happy together. She is even wearing specially-crafted, silver hands, which the king has made to improve the quality of her life.

After having become his husband and even growing pregnant, the woman is forced to endure a prolonged separation from him caused by his going off to war. During their time apart, the two send one another messages, which the Devil interferes with in a concerted effort to cause chaos and to destroy the majesty of their real and enduring romantic love. She has a child and lives in the castle. His mother has become a dear friend and, in fact, saves her from the Devil by refusing to murder her or the boy. Her son made no such demand whatsoever, but the Devil twisted the messenger so much as to cause that message to be delivered.

However, in rescuing the woman and the child, the king's mother sent the two away. They went and found further good fortune in the woodlands, where people took them in knowing the lady was a queen without her ever needing to tell them that.

Later, when her husband returned from his time at war, he learned about the mix up and was wracked with grief. He was very grateful to his mother for sparing them from the cruel, evil deceit that had ruthlessly corrupted his message of love for the wife and child; however, until his return, he had no idea of what had happened. Once he had accepted this, he set off to find his wife and son. The man searched seven years until at last he found them!

Even after such a length of time, the quality of their love remained steadfast; they found it was not possible for either to be simply replaced and they re-united joyfully. The quality of their lives was good. This doesn't mean that life was perfect at all times; it just means that they really loved one another, knew it and stayed together to the ends of their days.

The author focuses on the significance of the injuries sustained by the daughter. The father does to her what one version of the Skeleton Woman story explains her father did to her. She then sets out a series of events that quite clearly describe a process of initiation. Stage 1: The First Stage- The Bargain Without Knowing, 2: The Dismemberment, 3: The Wandering, 4: Finding Love in the Underworld, 5: The Harrowing of the Soul, 6: The Realm of the Wild Woman, 7: The Wild Bride and Bridegroom. These phases of growth and development make quite a journey. Gain, loss, redemption...The daughter's attitude towards adversity...The successful rebuking of the undesired followed by the success of true love....Followed by separation, then loss...then having a good attitude about moving forward as best one can given the circumstances...living with grief and sorrow...and then, long after all hope seemed to have been lost,...reunion and real happiness.

Chapter 15, Shadowing: Canto Hondo, The Deep Song Summary and Analysis

In this chapter, the author explores the behavior of shadowing and shows readers a variety of its functions. She uses wolves as a metaphor once again as she has much personal experience with them. The shadowing of wolves can be both impressive and frightening. What can be intimidating or anxiety provoking about it is that wolves, when shadowing form an invisible surveillance; they know how to survey a situation to determine whether or not they will be hunting or taking anything and how much of their pack will be needed to achieve this. What is beautiful about this, is that it involves information gathering through silence and invisibility. This is a case where a light touch is more effective than a heavier one. Many of us have had the experience of being startled when someone sneaks up on us. Often we jump and wonder, perhaps unconsciously, if we about to be harmed. Normally, our lives would not really be in danger, but the reality is that any animal or human of sufficient power has performed a powerful feat if able to approach another so closely without having been noticed.

Those who have been that light and silent know there is an ease and a kind of magic about it. This is a quality that can help lead women, whether as girls or women, back towards their own "wildish" selves. Of course, one can learn a great deal about nature's other animals. They are all so skittish, on the whole. Animals reveal themselves and hide from their opponents with a kind of sensitivity that is common among women and other humans at certain stages of their lives, but this behavior is often "scoffed at." This degree of awareness is highly valuable for the Wild Woman and her teachings.

The author expresses how much work there is for women as a group to do to move our culture forward, to continue to develop. She reiterates that in these chapters, she is creating something for all women. She is bringing work from the oral traditions into the written text to preserve it, to share it more widely, and to send it into the future. Part of this work, she refers to as reclamation. She tells readers that the original meaning of this is to call out so a hunting bird will return to the human it hunts with, not home to roost but back to the leather glove.

Estes refers to the power of dreams again in this chapter. In this case, she closely associates it with La Que Sabe, the One Who Knows. Dreams reveal messages sent by La Que Sabe. Estes advocates safeguarding the instincts of every individual woman. Part of her discourse concerns the predator, who is most strongly associated with a woman, either the father or lover. With the wisdom of La Que Sabe and the careful dismantling of naivete, girls can grow to be women, who let only the right men close and keep the predatory ones out, which is obviously easier to do when "father was not that way." Man, however, is no more prone to be the predator as is a live wolf or an angry mother creature, human or otherwise.

The author refocuses upon wolves as symbols for the psyche at the chapter's end. She provides a list of basic rules that women can use that can also be seen in reference to wolves. This is rather realistic and somewhat charming.

The book is approaching completion in this chapter. This may be part of the reason why she brings up other chapters late in this one. She encourages the readers to find where they do belong so they can experience the same joy as the swan rather than the awkwardness of the "outsider."

Chapter 16, The Wolf's Eyelash Summary and Analysis

This chapter contains an incredibly powerful story. Here a woman goes on an expedition into the wilds, but she has not really left the realms of human-dominated territory. This is apparent when she finds a wild wolf caught in a trap of human origin and design. The woman in the story was forced into the woods by some nascent, innate, powerful force. She was directed to head for the forest in order to renew her life so she could begin again, fresh and reborn. Having obeyed this wisdom, she makes her way to semi-wild lands, whereupon she makes the discovery of this wild animal.

She felt compassion for the animal and was herself not in the position of the hunter. She had no wish to destroy the beast and probably because she had no relationship with the hunters, there was nothing she could do except either leave the animal there, suffering in the manner that it was or else try to release it without getting killed or injured herself.

The wolf pleads to be rescued. She asks it: If I free you, will you harm me? After all; she's not all that naive and realizes that given the nature of wild animals, this is a touchy situation. The animal persuades her, mostly through pained yelping and howling to free it. She is rather an expert woodswoman, it turns out because not only does she free the wolf from the trap, but she then tends its wound.

To everyone's relief, the animal does not turn on her out of spite or indifference because she is human. Instead, the wolf grants her a precious gift that comes in a potent but humble package. It is a single body hair. This one, however, is an eyelash. They part on good terms.

When the woman returns from her wilderness excursion, it turns out that she is more than simply refreshed. She discovers over time that the eyelash of the wolf, when used as a talisman has unlocked a new power. She has acquired the power to sense motives. This one hair from the wild canine enables her to see others in ways that had been closed to her before. Thanks to its power, she is able to surround herself with kind and good people and is readily able to distinguish them from those who are not so nice. All this, without ever losing sight of the truth that a wolf is a wolf and can be trusted to behave like one.

With this powerful insight, Estes finishes the book. Now readers have traveled with her on quite a journey. The wolves, who are her favorite wild animal have turned up here and there as symbols, garnering at least some attention, albeit from a distance. Estes' hope is clear: that readers have found the joy of many stories they did not know before and greater access to wisdom within themselves and the world. She also hopes that the reader has found knowledge and insight through the discourse provided by the author.

Chapter 17, Afterward Story as Medicine Summary and Analysis

This is the result that comes to readers who had the equivalent of a standing ovation response to the main body of the work. She begins by bringing readers back to one of her original points. Stories are a special kind of medicine designed to be used as such.

This is where she begins to inform people once again of her own origins. Many of her people have a vibrant oral cultural tradition. Part of this culture, including in the present day, is to have individuals who have as a role official story teller for a given group of people.

Children are observed at times with the question in the elder's mind: Is this one a potential story teller? If you laughed, then you may have only heard this as a metaphor for picking out the liars in an assemblage of children. Everyone knows the little fibber just might be story teller material. An articulate and creative child is needed to grow into such a role. One who would be comfortable in public speaking. The author explains that the talent is easy enough to spot, once you know for what to look.

As an amendment to the above, Clarissa Pinkola Estes also lets readers know a bit more about psychological practice. She explains that such professionals are taught what not to do, perhaps even more than they are told what to do. All of this is part of their extensive training. There is some connection here to story telling. There are various reasons for sharing and telling stories. One purpose is medicine, and this is a bit different from entertainment. As such, the story teller learns about which story to tell when. This is part of a discernment process that involves the situation and those involved. Of course, stories also require the right audience. When used as medicine, the perfect story for a specific individual or group at the proper time will hold great power and be very useful.

Through this chapter, the author fills a gap left not entirely unaddressed but perhaps ineffectively addressed during the previous material. She shares a bit more about her personal work with readers and hopes to demonstrate how natural story tellers might see what they are by reading this part of her book. As already mentioned, it serves as and "encore" in a sense for those who want more. Lastly, it functions, or becomes a "tie in" to even more information that she provides in an addendum, followed by notes from the text. For those who have an academic relationship with the book or an intense interest in the subject matter, these final segments may well come in handy.

Important People

Clarissa Pinkola Estes

This is the book's author. She describes herself as a Latina with a mixed heritage. She happily claims to have a rather worldly outlook, which was strongly encouraged by her upbringing. She is formally educated, with not only a doctoral degree but holds a certificate with respect to her specially-formulated, post-doctoral work.

She offers readers still more of her credentials. She is a specialist in Jungian psychology. That is one reason why she is especially well prepared for writing about the Wild Woman archetype. Jung's almost entire focus was the archetype and how it influences people in real life. For Jung, as it probably also is for her, archetypes involve psychology in a way that, while true for individuals, goes far beyond the individual. The roots and branches of archetypes are from diverse sources--ethnic roots, daily life, the history of the pre-urban or even contemporary rural life.

She also assures readers that she knows well how to use archetypes for personal healing on the emotional and mental levels. While this can protect and heal the overt physical conditions of someone, she specializes in these other areas. Her type or therapy can be preparatory or initiatory or one of healing. Archetypes are quite special in that they provide directions for growth, but they exist in terms of self-awareness as much as societal roles.

Baba Yaga

This is the Wild Woman as the wise old woman, in some traditions called the Crone. She appears early in the book. She initiates a much younger one, named Vasalisa. She is depicted as old, ugly, very intimidating and extremely powerful. A girl child, who is mature within the range of childhood, is sent off to meet this Old Lady, by malicious step relatives, who wish to end her life. However they have masked their utter malice by couching their wish in the language of sending her upon a quest with a task to find the family another source of fire so they can re-light their family hearth.

Baba Yaga harbors all manner of wisdom and insight, knowledge and skills. She provides discipline and basic training for adulthood by making the girl work in exchange for what she has asked. Of course, this makes it available to the girl despite her lack of money. The Baba Yaga is very magical but also extremely realistic. This shows because her house rests upon chicken legs, and the Old Woman is able to fly around in a large iron cooking pot, i.e. a cauldron.

Even though she is no cutesy Grandma, Baba Yaga is protective as well as educational. She sends the girl back on her way with what she asked for but headed up with its own intimidating power, which resides inside a skull atop a stick. The young one now walks with a staff and has a fire-bearing skull.

Spider Woman

This is one of the names of an especially-sacred woman found in Native American traditions. The Spider Woman has transformative and healing powers. She turns up in the early stories in the book. She is the most other-worldly of the forms of the Wild Woman presented so far.

La Que Sabe

This is "The One Who Knows." As the name suggests, she is from the Latin tradition. This tradition is from the Americas, more so than from Spain. She turns up throughout the book being apparently one of the favorites of the author. She is the Wild Woman in the form of a wizard: the powerful and wise old lady. As the One Who Knows, she is able to assist others in gaining knowledge and wisdom.

Skeleton Woman

Skeleton Woman is all about the Life/Death/Life cycle. She is terrifying and deeply sad. This is quite understandable when the readers learn that in some versions of the story, she was literally killed by her own father, but in other cases maimed by him. The author tells at least one tale about her near the center of the book.

The author uses her to enhance the readers' understanding of this Life/Death/Life cycle. In the case of Skeleton Woman, it involves the difference, the Death and the rebirth of woman through the total destruction of the kind of connection that first formed her: her father's sexual connection with her mother, then her Death for having been a "naughty" girl, and then later her rebirth into Life when she finds herself restored and re-invigorated through a loving intimate relationship with a man.

Neither the man nor the woman expected this. He was innocently fishing only to discover the sheer terror of a skeletal murder victim, and then he was unable to escape the remains. After he surrenders to his inability to escape, he sets her in order, attends to her and when he relaxes enough to rest himself, she comes to life and becomes his companion.

Vasalisa

Vasalisa is a young girl from one of the earlier stories. She is the one who is sent to Baba Yaga and instead of failing and dying as the step family had planned, she makes it all the way there and receives initiation. She suffers. She represents the hard childhood in contrast to the easy, idyllic one.

This is a child who has suffered a very real tragedy that holds aloft the dangers of Death tied up with the Life giving powers of women. Her mother died while she was a child. The mother managed to leave her daughter with a message. The child made the most of this help and lived through her and her father's grief at the mother's death. The child suffers the disappointment that the step relatives may have been fine for her father but were not doing her any good at all.

Hidalgo

This isn't a name in itself so much as the title. This is a man who is La Llorono's lover. He is also the father of two sons of hers. For some years they are together. Then he decides to return to Spain and marry someone who has been chosen for him by his family.

La Llorono is quite distraught when he expresses his intention to abandon her and take their children from her back to his parents. In some of the La Llorono tales, the mother of his sons kills them instead of allowing them to be taken away. Hidalgo is perhaps the archetype of the man who is never able to leave his mother/family and transfer his loyalties to his female lover; instead, he abandons the lover when the family calls him home.

The Little Match Girl

This is the lead character of a fairy tale that has a sad ending. She is an orphan or a runaway. This unsupervised child is endeavoring to make her way in the world. She has succeeded in doing more than nothing for herself. She has built herself a shelter in a relatively safe place. She has even found a way to bring herself a little money. There is a basic difficulty. Every child who has been taught how to make a good fire and every adult who knows how to do this will not be able to avoid seeing the giant gap in the girl's knowledge. Even though she has found some matches, she lacks the added security of having any fire making skills or a real fire.

There is something else obviously missing. Something has kept her from adult assistance. As a result, the child in the fairy tale dies, freezing to death after the last flickering light of her matches fades away.

Zeus

This Olympian deity is mentioned in Clarissa's book. In this case, he shows up as "the bad guy." He casts his own son out of Olympus because the boy stuck up for his mother, who is Zeus's opponent in this argument.

Hephaestus

The son of the god Zeus and goddess Hera, he is an Olympian. Despite being one of the Grecian Olympian gods, he finds that his deific parents are not above arguing among themselves. In this case, he not only agrees with his mother but takes sides and works from her side of the situation.

He is reminded that he is weaker and less powerful than his father when his father casts him down and out of Olympus. He is granted his own realm below, where his great smithing skills will prosper and, despite his ugliness, he will win fame and respect.

Hera

A goddess of Mount Olympus, a Grecian divine realm. She has a husband-consort, whose name is Zeus. Even though they are deities and not mere mortals, some of their behavior is virtually identical to that of mortals including the fact that they tend to argue with each other. In this case, she and her husband are having a disagreement.

Her son steps agrees with her, and there are major consequences. She continues to argue and may have lost. Her helpful son is banished by her husband from Olympus either because his support was so powerful and/or because even the two of them together were not powerful enough to stop her husband.

pollutant

This comes up in its plural form later in the book, particularly in reference to La Llorona. It is something that has a poisoning effect, rather than being truly nourishing or healthy.

traps

These are talked about in the chapter on self-preservation. In this context, they are intentionally used with an analogy or metaphor comparing them to traps set for animals.

The Devil

Famous for being God's adversary and former "right hand man," the Devil makes at least two appearances during the book. The author does not go into how noticeable it is that the Devil, in his famous confrontation with God met with a very similar fate to the one Zeus meted out to his son, Hephaestus: Down and out he goes, to get his very own realm within which to exercise the power that truly is his own.

Once the Devil turns up in disguise as an old soldier when he "does something" to the girl's new red shoes when she wears them to church and then starts dancing. All he did was tap on the bottoms of them.

Stories later, the miller makes a business deal that will finally rescue his family from a poverty that has befallen them. At first believing that he made a very good deal, he soon learns that he has made what is a dreadful mistake, but he cannot undo what has been done, so the family does their best to live with the consequences. In good news, despite the hardships created by the Devil's interest in taking the daughter as part of the bargain, he fails to do so. This ironically is in keeping with father's original intentions in making the deal when he had not planned on letting the Devil have his daughter. The family got out of the deal in a roundabout way, despite the Devil's tricks, but it wasn't easy, and the girl ended up a cripple, maimed by her own father in an attempt to please the Devil because of the bargain.

The Devil tries to interfere with this same girl later; his wish to possess, control or to destroy her fail miserably, but his efforts are very effective in causing her very serious difficulties. The devil's later meddling causes a seven-year separation between herself and their child with her husband, although they eventually reunite.

Brak

This is "the ice man." There is a story late in the book in which he commits a murder out of anger, which stems from unrequited love. In the story, he is, in fact, made of ice and so is the icicle with which he kills. Within 24 hours, there is nothing left of either the weapon or him. Both have been melted to water.

Objects/Places

The Cave

This is where La Loba "sings over the bones" in the first story of the book. It is an older woman; she may be an old single, menopausal woman or a woman who has a mate who is not present at the time of the telling.

The cave is hers. It is a natural, strong shelter in the wild. It is a special location. Powerful natural magic takes place. It contains the power of the woman inside, but she is not trapped in any way shape or form.

Wolf Bones

These go along with the cave. They occur in the first story. La Loba gathers them together to her cave wherein she performs a resurrection along with a joyous celebration of life through the power of her own singing. However, the impression is that she could not do this without the actual bones of the wolf.

Blue Beard

This object has been retained by a cloister of nuns. It is the remnant of a powerful man who is of exceptional danger to women. He was a danger to other men by virtue of being a warrior, but his aggression against his wives, who were not warriors, tended to be dangerous or deadly.

It is only through the violence of other men that the man with the blue beard is defeated in his aggression against his sequence of wives. It is only due to the sufficiently early awareness of his newest and quite young wife and her sisters that his deadly nature was notices soon enough to have him defeated, instead of another woman ending up dead.

There is no explanation as to why his beard is kept by nuns, who live together in seclusion, mainly for reasons of mutual aid and protection.

Skeleton

The skeletal remains of a murdered/killed woman. The skeleton is safe from decay at the bottom of a body of water.

Treasure

This object is from the story Skeleton Woman. It is cause for well-placed hope of some kind.

Jail Walls

In the chapter devoted to the search for belonging, the author tells readers that women's longing to help along the wild soul- and she means this in a healthy way - will lead women to "paint the sky on jail walls" (p.188).

The Netherlands

This location comes up in the chapter that includes the famous story of "The Ugly Duckling". This creature is saved by others who are not of like kind and has a very rough time among them until making the drastic transition into a swan.

Poisoned Baits

They provide something needed but have something nasty and terribly unhealthy closely connected with them or even as part of them.

Sealskin

This is in chapter 9. Belonging to a seal-woman, the seal-woman sheds her skin when she comes out of the water and becomes her human aspect. She must have her skin in order to reemerge into her seal aspect. The man, who becomes her husband, hides her skin in order to force the woman to stay in her human form and marry him. The woman's son later finds the skin and returns it to her so that she can become her other aspect, that of a seal.

Lakota

The name of a tribe of Native Americans that can be currently found in locations such as Indiana.

Foot Prints

These are marks in the ground made by feet or footwear but only when the ground is soft enough. These are referred to in chapter 9.

Silver Hands

These were made by an underworld king for the handless maiden who became his wife.

Doe's Tongue and Eyeballs

These were substituted in order for a woman to provide fake evidence of a murder. What is incredible is that this was all falsehood that came as a healthy response to a lie.

Themes

Wild Woman Archetype

One theme of this book is to help women to understand the Wild Woman archetype. Part of how Estes does this is to share numerous stories she has culled from ethnically diverse sources. Readers meet at least one form of the Wild Woman in nearly every story. The guises are not all the same.

This is one of the features of an archetype. It shows up in the culture through diverse forms. Archetypes are very much like principles in the respect that the same one can appear in a variety of stories and guises. In fact, it is only through these different examples that readers will cultivate a sense for perceiving the truth.

Another feature of an archetype is that they are not 2-dimensional. Much like life, or beyond life, each archetype can be viewed as being more than just an image or each expression of what it respresents. However, one is readily able to grasp living forms of the archetype whether observing it in others or through self-imaging.

The Wild Woman is presented much more than the "wild girl," but the author does show how there is a connection between the two. There are stories of how a given girl is initiated and goes up to a new level of functioning in the world. These initiations come with experience and are as real as a child's movement through educational grade levels in the school systems. The child/girl changes as she goes through the grade levels.

By the end of the book, women should be better prepared to relocate or to tap into this archetypal energy at will. They will be able to find and nurture this power within themselves as well discern it when it appears as a young woman, or Mother, or Wise Old Lady.

Psychological Healing for Women

One of the primary functions of this book is to assist women in individual healing and to empower women throughout the culture to heal "as a group," the whole group of women in the nation and the world.

The least pleasant part of this process is that Estes describes for readers a number of different problems that women may have heard of, or known friends who suffered from, or experienced themselves. They may run into some such difficulties in the future. For women feeling and being healthy and strong, it is a lot like reading about illness. However, none of this is presented in the manner of scientific prose. This being the case, the over all tenor of this theme is one of commiserating friends or of confidantes.

The helpful part comes with following how the author points up trouble spots in women's psychological lives. She does this partly through reference to her own practice as a professional psychologist, but this is not the only way that she does. She shows readers through interpretation how to use wisdom from these stories to heal their need to reconnect with some aspect of the soul or the psyche that has gone too long unattended.

Of course, the author never suggests that her book is a substitute for professional mental health care. What she does do is offer cultural ways that protect the woman from psychological harm and equips women to be able to offer helpful advice or encouragement or nurturing to each other from some of these stories.

One potent definition that she offers readers is the difference between comfort and nurturing. Estes differentiates between fantasy coping, rooted in ideas of helplessness (whether the helplessness is real or false),and taking actions to effectively remedy a situation, especially if it is actually life threatening. Comfort and coping go together. She shows this by telling readers that if there is a plant trapped in a dark closet and you go in and give it a little water and talk to it, then leave it there, you have given comfort. However, if you go in there and take the plant and put it someplace where there is sunlight and then water it and talk to it, you have nurtured it.

Through the story of the Little Match Box Girl, Estes shows that fantasizing under life-threatening conditions when one can take some action to change the situation is lethal and dangerous. When there really is no hope, it might not be a mistake to fantasize. However, when there is, what is needed is to figure out how to make life work, to solve the problem, instead of ruining hope by handling it badly. The trouble with the Match Box Girl was that she did not apply her mind to solving her trouble. Instead of either finding fuel and making herself a hot fire to save her life, or finding a way to be cared for by adults who would teach her twhat she needed to know, she stayed in a "fantasy" world, which resulted in her death.

Reworking Oral Traditions for a Global Culture

Clarissa Pinkola Estes writes that she herself has a poly-ethnic background. This is quite common in America and in other nations who have a tradition of liberal immigration policies. Often, the cultural and political landscapes go together.

The author cites that throughout the world, there continue to be many cultural traditions relating to oral story telling. Many a liar has been called a story teller, and there are jokes about how one has to have a combination of truthfulness with a certain amount of being a "liar" to be a good story teller. However stories told as part of a longstanding tradition may well have strict limits for dishonesty. Traditions vary. There are traditions when recounting a story exactly by traditioin is absolutely vital. In other cases, there is some leeway, and there are cases when it is acceptable within the tradition itself to embellish an existing story. The latter case is observed in this book in relation the La Llorono story. Estes relates one of the oldest and most traditional versions that she knows but then also shares with readers how many more versions of this story she has encountered. A few may go back in time quite a ways, but several are delightfully recent in their emergence.

The continuance of La Llorono into new forms is a strong indicator of a vigorous story and a healthy oral tradition within whatever culture or subculture it develops and thrives. There is another feature of the cultural realms in which this story lives, however. It may be that the story telling is unregulated. There are traditions where there is a distinctive role of tribal or group story teller. In these cases, memorizing numerous, specific tales and passing them on as diligently as one passes down scientific or practical knowledge is highly valued and closely watched.

The author really touches the proverbial tip of the iceberg when she shares fairy tales that have remained unaltered and others that have transformed over generations. Estes introduces people to this topic and incorporates her stories entirely by the theme of her book. She really just opens what she herself might call a door on this realm. The world's story telling traditions are rich, varied, and some have some simple and other complex systems. For those passionate about the subject, this book makes a good primer to an amazing world.

Although this is not the only theme in the book, it is certainly an important one. So much of the author's work on women's psychology is done here through sharing the cultural history of tales. Her interpretive techniques can be about which values are being maintained and which changed. For example, in the Red Shoes, the fairy tale ends with the dancer having her feet cut off to get her to serve others, showing that a selfish lifestyle will not be tolerated and would turn from something joyous into an evil if not curtailed. However, the way that such a set of conditions would be handled at this stage in our history and in this culture for women has changed; this shows clearly in the way that Estes interprets the story in relation to women's health en masse. She tells us to heed the warning signs, but to be willing to work to rescue that original part of the girl on a deeper and healthier level.

Style

Perspective

The author is both a worldly and well-educated woman. Because of this, she is able to add personal experience as an individual but also as a practitioner of psychotherapy. She writes from the perspective as an expert healer of the mind, or if readers prefer, as a woman who has the power to unleash the self-healing powers of the minds of others.

The author is an American and a Latina. This gives her insight into understanding these stories. She has had access to European and Hispanic tales, as well as other information from the indigenous peoples of North America.

The author writes the book with a qualitatively-personalized narrative voice. However, she also includes and recounts stories with the third person narrative form. She provides transference of the oral tradition by passing on versions of fairy tales and other cultural visions that she did not invent.

Tone

This book has multiple purposes. Readers sense the author's personality coming through, which is not only acceptable but welcome within this context. The language is relatively simple, although not simplistic. Presumably, given the education level of the author, this is to facilitate accessibility to the widest possible readership. While it is sad that she has not made use of more complex prose, it is fabulous that she has made the work clear and comprehensible to many women of various educational levels.

Another purpose of this book is to educate readers, who are interested in learning more about the "wild woman archetype." The contents are clearly laid out for informal learning, although the book could be used as a textbook for a university course.

The tone is light enough to serve as entertainment for those not interested in it as a means of self-help and/or growth.

Finally, there is a comfortable combination of objectivity and subjectivity. Readers will get the feeling that the author wrote this book partly to share her own viewpoints, rather than only expressing those of others. She has indicated to readers the extent of her credentials and experience and yet it is quite clear that this is not a work designed for a journal of psychiatric medicine but hopefully would be of interest to some of those who would read such journals. However, such professionals will likely read this work on Saturday or sneak bits of it during their lunch break.

Structure

The book is divided into a series of chapters. In each chapter, there is some discourse and at least one story. The discourse and story are designed to mutually enhance one another.

The book progresses in a natural manner. By the middle of the book, one has so adapted to the way that the author has put the chapters together that there is the expectation that the next chapters will be similarly arragned, but not without some flexibility.

The book's structure seems to suit the author's purposes. The feeling of the book is comfortable. For those interested in more details or a more academic approach, she has placed a well-organized set of notes at the back end of the nonfiction work.

Quotes

"Vasalisa entered the house feeling triumphant, for she had survived her dangerous journey and brought fire back to her home. But the skull on the stick watched the stepsisters' and stepmother's every move and burnt into them, and by morning it had burnt the wicked trio to cinders." p. 76

"For Wild Woman it helps if the lover is just a little bit 'psychic' to, a person who can 'see into' her heart." p.106

"She has a big pot; she moves through the sky in a cauldron." p. 328

"So, living as we do in a world that requires both meditative and outward action, I find it very useful to utilize the concept of a masculine nature or animus in woman. In proper balance animus acts as helper, helpmate, lover, brother, father, king," p. 312

"Begin; this is how to clear the polluted river. If you're scared scared to fail I say begin already, fail if you must, pick yourself up, start again. If you fail again, so what? Begin again. It is not the failure that holds us back but the reluctance to begin over again that causes us to stagnate." p.317

"...as in the offhanded." p. 316

"Negative complexes are particularly attracted to the juiciest ideas, the most revolutionary and wonderful ideas and the most rampant forms of creativity." p. 316

"Elysium is described as a place of perpetual day, where souls may elect to be reborn on earth whenever they please." p. 415.

"... Life/Death/Life..." p. 415.

"Overkill through excesses, or excessive behaviors, is acted out by women who are famished for a life that has meaning and makes sense for them." p. 230.

"Psychologically, Jung speculated that the instincts derived from the psychoid unconscious, that layer of psyche where biology and spirit might touch. I am of a considered same mind, and would go further to venture that the creative instinct in particular is as much the lyrical language of the Self as is the symbology of dreams." p. 231.

"A woman is born with all instinct intact." p. 231.

"When Skeleton Woman uses the fisherman's heart, she uses the central motor of the entire pysche, the only thing that really matters now the only thing capable of producing pure and innocent feeling." p. 156

"Yet, over and over perhaps since the beginning of infinity, those who would be her mate are not quite sure they comprehend her true nature." p. 112.

"So, finally the little dog raced back to the sisters' hut again, and this time the sisters were readying themselves to be wed." p. 113.

"There is a specific pattern of the loss of instinct. It is essential study this pattern, to actually memorize it, so that we can guard the treasures of our basic natures and those of our daughters as well." p. 213.

Topics for Discussion

Which of the forms of the Wild Woman is your favorite? Explain your answer.

Describe your own Wild Woman for the stage of life you are in now. Make sure that it is realistically accurate, yet be sure to free your mind to work archetypal energy into the vision.

Name one place in the book where you agree with the author's interpretation of a story. Then, also note another where you have a different interpretation. Describe the lesson that is most evident to you in that case. Show why you disagree with the author.

How do you feel the "Wild Woman" appears in urban culture?

Describe what most frightens you about Wild Woman and what you most love about her.

Do you feel the author's work is healing in nature? Answer yes/no followed by a description or explanation of why or why not.

Summarize how the author relates to wolves. Then, describe your own feelings about wolves, including the presence or lack of familiarity with them.

Are you able to see the "wildish" woman in others?

Compare and contrast the Old Woman in the forms of Baba Yaga and the Old Lady who takes in the girl in the story of the Red Shoes.

The wolves are the author's favorite animal: pick one of your favorite wild animals and describe why you like it and if possible what it is about it that causes you to have a kinship feeling.

List five attributes of the Wild Woman during the mother phase that you feel are healthy for women. List another five that express why you love civilization.

Discuss how the stories that involve both children educate women about learning and about teaching and guarding our young.

Made in the USA
Middletown, DE
18 December 2017